LIFE CHOICES

TRUSTING GOD IN LIFE'S DECISIONS AND CHALLENGES

God

Family

Friends

Sex and Dating

JIM BRITTS

TO SAVE A LIFE

OUTREⱯCH®

Life Choices **Small Group Leader's Guide**
Copyright © 2010 by Jim Britts
Published by Outreach, Inc., in partnership with New Song Pictures.

Outreach, Inc., Vista, CA
OutreachPublishing.com

Cover Design: Tim Downs
Interior Design: Alexia Wuerdeman
Editing: Toni Ridgaway and Jennifer Dion

Printed in the United States of America

ISBN: 978-1-9355-4116-5

TABLE OF CONTENTS

A NOTE FROM THE AUTHOR

A NOTE FROM THE AUTHOR

Hey! My name is Jim, and I'm the screenwriter of the film *To Save A Life*. Like you, I work with teenagers. I was really blown away by the response to the first **To Save A Life** curriculum—in my own ministry and from the thousands of groups around the world that joined us in it. If you did the study, my guess is your students are a lot more willing to regularly share what is really going on in their lives, and they love to be empowered to help others. Based on that response, we decided to introduce a second curriculum, which you're holding in your hands right now.

The heart behind the film and both curriculums is simply this, "You're never more like Jesus than when you are reaching out to the hurting and lonely." You really can't go a page in the Gospels without Jesus either reaching out to those who most people ignore, or challenging His disciples to do the same. In **Life Choices**, we go more in depth with several of the difficult issues and choices your students face on a regular basis. The intent is to help teens deal with these issues biblically, then to empower them to help others who are struggling in the same way.

Below are some suggestions that should help your small group benefit from this powerful series. Some of these suggestions might seem obvious to you, but I want to make sure every **Life Choices** small group leader is equipped, regardless of whether you are a veteran youth worker or a what-did-I-get-myself-into "newbie."

1) BE A SHEPHERD, NOT A SMALL GROUP LEADER.

Although the cover of this book reads, "Small Group Leader's Guide," the word the Bible uses for what you're doing is "shepherd." Here are some ways I think the two roles differ.

- Small group leaders make a commitment to lead a discussion. Shepherds make a commitment to help students grow and become more like Jesus.

- Small group leaders think it's their responsibility to teach the group. Shepherds know that a good leader does more listening than talking.

- Small group leaders hope everyone in their group will show up. Shepherds are in close communication with their students and are not surprised by their attendance.

- Small group leaders are content with their group just showing up. Shepherds constantly encourage, challenge, and pray for their students.

- Small group leaders believe the group had a good session when there was a good discussion. Shepherds have a good night when their students are each taking steps in spiritual growth.

- Small group leaders pray for their students occasionally. Shepherds pray a ton, because they know the Holy Spirit is the only One who can truly help their students grow spiritually.

2) COME PREPARED EACH WEEK.

Before your group meeting, spend at least 30 minutes reviewing the videos and questions. I've intentionally included too many questions so that you can easily fill one-to-two hours. Also, pray for your group and your meeting; ask God to give you wisdom and discernment as you lead.

3) DO THE DAILY LESSONS.

If the students in your group don't know how to feed themselves spiritually by having a daily quiet time and reading their Bible, they will most likely drop their faith once they graduate from high school. One of the most important things students should learn is how to "hear" God's voice by reading their Bible. Guess who MUST set an example by having a daily quiet time and reading the Bible? YOU!

4) GET TO KNOW YOUR STUDENTS' PARENTS.

The truth is that you only get a small amount of time each week with your students, but their parents see them throughout the week. Real life change will happen when you are working with your students' parents, not competing against them. Consider inviting parents to come to your group one night so they know what you're doing.

5) GET RID OF ALL DISTRACTIONS.

The Bible says, "Be still and know that I am God." This verse is harder than ever to apply, thanks to cell phones, texting, MP3 players, and the Internet. When your group starts, ask your students to take all their electronic devices (and anything else that might distract them) and place them in a basket in another room.

6) STAY CONNECTED TO THE WHOLE YOUTH MINISTRY.

If you are not the head youth leader at your church, then make sure you frequently share with that person regarding your group and the progress of your students. Before sharing, remember that maintaining your group's confidentiality is crucial, and be careful not to share anything a student would consider confidential or sensitive (although suspected abuse, self-injury, or suicidal thoughts are exceptions*). As a youth pastor, I think it's incredibly honoring when small group leaders give me updates.

If you have questions about handling particularly difficult issues, see Handling the Tough Stuff in the back of this guide.

7) HAVE YOUR STUDENTS GET A *LIFE CHOICES* STUDENT GUIDE.

I highly recommend that each of your teens get a Student Guide. Because some of the issues included in **Life Choices** are delicate and complicated, students will get the most out of the study if they can record their most personal thoughts and feelings in their own book. Having a Student Guide will also allow them to go back and review what they've learned. In addition, the Student Guide will help them learn how to read the Bible and find answers for their day-to-day decisions and challenges.

8) SEE THE MOVIE—TOGETHER!

Even though there are five weeks in this study, it's really designed to take six weeks to complete. For the first week, I strongly encourage you to watch **To Save A Life** as a group, and encourage your students to bring their friends. After the movie, remember to invite any visitors to come back for the **Life Choices** study, so they can truly live out the movie's themes for the following five weeks.

Oh, and one last thing...thank you so much for pouring your life into a group of teenagers. Hopefully you already know this, but WHAT YOU'RE DOING REALLY MATTERS. You will experience some powerful times together and learn some compelling truths through this small group, but more than anything your students just need...you! Love them, listen to them, encourage the heck out of them, and every chance you get, show them Jesus through your words and actions.

Jim

(screenwriter of *To Save A Life*)

HOW TO USE YOUR
SMALL GROUP
LEADER'S GUIDE

HOW TO USE YOUR SMALL GROUP LEADER'S GUIDE

This Small Group Leader's Guide will provide the framework for your group meetings. The guide includes step-by-step instructions for each meeting, a full list of discussion questions and short teachings, plus a weekly challenge for your students. There might be more discussion questions than most groups can handle in the time you have available, but I know seventh-grade boys can whip through material a lot faster than sophomore girls. So, if you find yourself pressed for time, feel free to use only the questions that are most relevant to your group.

Your *Life Choices* **Resource DVD** includes one *To Save A Life* movie clip and one short video teaching from me for each week. The instructions in the weekly section of this guide will tell you when to play each video.

Between meetings, the guide offers six daily devotionals, designed to get you reading the Bible and spending time with God every day. The devotionals in your guide are identical to the devotionals in the Student Guide. As I mentioned before, one of the best ways to lead is to lead by example. Faithfully completing the daily Bible studies will put you in a position to discuss the lessons with your students. Plus, the daily routine will help you set aside time to be alone with God and receive His encouragement and wisdom.

Each of the daily Bible studies will practice the five "Rs" that will allow God to feed you (and your students) through His Word:

RELAX

We live in a really noisy world. There are so many voices running through our brains (friends, teenagers, significant others, senior pastors) that it's easy to miss what God's trying to tell us. So before you open your Bible to begin your study, close your eyes and just relax. Take a couple deep breaths and ask God to remove all of the other voices in your head, so you can hear what He has to say. Don't rush through this time; take at least a minute or two to relax and focus on the study.

READ

In this section of the study, you will be instructed to look up and read the Bible text for the day. Have a pen with you so that you can underline whatever stands out to you and make a note of anything you don't understand.

REACT

When you have a talk with a friend, you want them to react to what you say; it shows they're listening and that they care about you and what you're telling them. God is the same way. He loves to speak to us personally, and then He looks forward to hearing what we think about what we're learning from Him. Failing to somehow respond to what you read is a sure-fire way to numb your heart to God's voice. So, in this section of the study, you will have a chance to record your thoughts about the day's devotional.

RELATE

The goal is not really for you to go through the Bible—it's more important for the Bible to go through you. James 1:22 says, "Do not merely listen to the word and so deceive yourself. *Do what it says.*" So this section of the study gives you the opportunity to apply what you've learned in a practical way.

RESPOND

The primary way God speaks to us is through the Bible; the primary way we talk back to Him is through prayer. This section is your chance to thank God for what He's taught you that day and to ask for strength to live it out. Some people find it very helpful to write their prayers out, and there's space provided in this section for this.

GLOW

Matthew 5:16 reads, "Let your light shine before men that they might see your good deeds and praise your father in heaven." When we read the Bible every day and spend time with God, He can be a light through us. This section will help you think about how you can "glow" with God's light and live out the week's lesson in your world.

STARTING THE *LIFE CHOICES* STUDY

- Meet with your youth ministry or small group on a weekly basis to listen to (or watch) the teaching, answer the discussion questions, and pray with your group members.

- After your group meeting, complete one devotional each day. These devotionals will help you practice **Relaxing** in God's presence, **Reading** a Bible passage, **Reacting** to what you read, **Relating** to God's Word by applying it to your life, and **Responding** to God in prayer.

- On the day of your group meeting, complete the weekly **Glow** section to record your experience with the past week's devotionals. This section will also prepare you to offer a challenge or inspiring story to your group.

THE REAL
AUTHORS

THE REAL AUTHORS

As we study the very relevant issues in *Life Choices*, we're going to look in the Bible at stories of people who were just like us. They laughed like us, went through pain like us, and even had doubts and questions about spiritual things…like us. Here is a little background on some of them:

King David:

David was known as "a man after God's own heart." He killed lions, bears, and giants in his spare time. He was the youngest of eight brothers and could play the harp. He wrote almost half of the book of Psalms, but was also *far from* perfect.

King Solomon:

He was the son of King David and the richest and wisest man ever to live. He wrote Proverbs, Ecclesiastes, and Song of Solomon. He had a very intimate relationship with God but definitely knew what it was like to live with regret. He made a lot of mistakes but is living proof that God can redeem our worst decisions in life.

Apostle Paul:
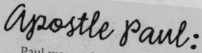

Paul was probably the most passionate Christian ever born. He went from being a persecutor of Christians to someone willing to die for Jesus. He wrote more than half of the books in the New Testament (many from a prison cell), planted tons of churches, and would say that among all sinners, he was the worst. He carried a lot of pain but helped a lot of people.

Jesus:

The Son of God and Creator of the Universe who came down to the earth to die for your sins. He saved mankind and desperately wants a relationship with you. (He doesn't really need much more of an introduction than that.)

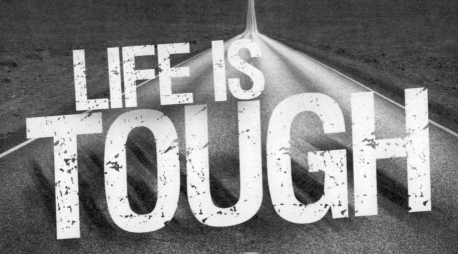

LIFE IS
TOUGH

PURPOSE

To shatter the myth that a person's life has to appear perfect before they walk through the doors of a church. In fact, church is the perfect place to be when life is falling apart.

KEY SCRIPTURES

James 1:2–4; John 16:33

OPEN YOUR GROUP MEETING WITH PRAYER.

WEEKLY SCENARIO

Explain to your group, "Each week, I'm going to give you a hypothetical scenario, and then I'm going to ask you to give advice in response to it. Each scenario will be based on something that happens in real life, and I want you to think about the advice you'd give the person in the situation. The topic for tonight is Life Is Tough."

Read the Week 1 scenario aloud, then ask your students to give advice to the person described in the scenario.

"My life is pretty tough right now. My only two real friends both transferred to another school this past fall, leaving me totally alone during lunch. I wish I could approach some people and ask if I can sit with them, but I'm as introverted as you can get. Even the thought of doing that feels like decapitation with a plastic knife. On top of all this, my parents are fighting more than ever, and I don't think they are going to make it. What should I do?"

⬤ MOVIE TIME

Watch the **Week 1 movie clip** on your *Life Choices* Resource DVD.

MY WHOLE LIFE IS FALLING APART

In this scene, Jake shares his frustration with Chris, saying that this "whole God thing" doesn't seem to be working.

"Jake, God's not some genie, or a vending machine, and He's not worth it because He makes your life all better."
– Chris to Jake in To Save A Life

Ask the group to respond to the movie clip by answering the questions below.

- What stood out to you in this movie clip? Was there anything you learned?
- Is there anything in this clip that applies to your life as well?

Before starting the discussion questions, have all your group members complete "My Life" in the Week 1 section of their Student Guide. At the same time, you fill out "My Life" on the following page in this guide.

If one or more of your group members does not have a Student Guide, you can read "My Life" out loud from your own guide and have your group members write their answers on a separate sheet of paper.

My Life

The truth is that all of us have tough issues that affect our lives. Look at the issues listed below; are there any that currently apply to your life? Choose one or two issues, and then fill in the rest of the sentence.

1) FAMILY ISSUES: LIVING IN MY FAMILY IS TOUGH RIGHT NOW BECAUSE...

_____

_____

_____

2) FRIEND ISSUES: LIFE IS TOUGH WITH MY FRIENDS RIGHT NOW BECAUSE...

_____

_____

_____

3) GUY/GIRL ISSUES: LIFE IS TOUGH WITH MY BOYFRIEND/GIRLFRIEND BECAUSE...

_____

_____

_____

4) IDENTITY ISSUES: I'M STRUGGLING WITH WHO I AM BECAUSE....

_____

_____

_____

5) ADDICTION ISSUES: LIFE IS TOUGH BECAUSE I JUST CAN'T SEEM TO STOP....

_____

_____

_____

6) FORGIVENESS ISSUES: I'M HAVING A HARD TIME FORGIVING SOMEONE BECAUSE....

_____

_____

_____

7) STRESS ISSUES: LIFE FEELS SO OVERWHELMING BECAUSE....

_____

_____

_____

8) LIFE ISSUES: LIFE IS JUST PLAIN TOUGH RIGHT NOW BECAUSE....

_____

_____

_____

DISCUSSION QUESTIONS

1. Share one of the happiest moments you have ever had. What made it so great?

2. Share one of the toughest moments you have ever had. What made it so difficult?

Leader, share the following with your group:

✗ "The truth is that everybody will go through difficult times in life. In John 16:33, Jesus says, 'I have told you these things, so that in me you may have peace. In this world you will have trouble. But take heart! I have overcome the world.' When we choose to follow God, He never promises us a problem-free life. What He does promise is peace if we choose to deal with our problems in the right way."

3. Complete this sentence: "One of the issues I marked down on the 'My Life' page was…"

4. Complete this sentence: "I normally deal with this issue by…"

5. Complete this sentence: "My current way of dealing with this issue has been successful/unsuccessful because…"

Leader, share the following:

✗ "There are different ways to deal with the difficult stuff in our lives. Tonight, we're going to spend time in the Bible looking at some of those ways."

DENIAL: *READ 2 SAMUEL 11:1-5 AND 12:1-6.*

6. How does David respond to the problems he's facing? How have you seen people today try to brush difficult things under the rug and pretend like they don't exist? What do you think are some of the consequences of using denial to deal with difficult issues?

BLAME GAME: *READ LUKE 10:38-42.*

7. In this story, Martha began to grow bitter because she was doing all the work while her sister seemed to be relaxing. How does Martha finally react? How do people today blame others when

life doesn't go as planned? What do you think are some of the consequences of dealing with life's tough times in this manner?

GIVE UP: *READ MATTHEW 27:1-5.*

8. How does Judas respond to the tough things he is facing in his life? What are some other ways in which people today give up when stuff gets hard? What do you think are some of the consequences of giving up during tough times?

TRUST GOD AND KEEP GOING: *READ GENESIS 39:1-23.*

9. Sometimes bad stuff happens in our lives, but it's not always our fault. In this story, Joseph really did nothing wrong but still had to go through some tough stuff. Share examples of how people can turn to God during tough times. What are some consequences or benefits of trusting God during tough times?

10. Which of these four methods do you usually use when going through tough stuff? Can you share an example?

11. What do you think is the best method for dealing with pain in your life?

READ PSALM 107:13-44.

Leader, share the following:

"God hears your cries when you are troubled. He is the God of the hurting, lonely, left out, and lost. God doesn't waste pain; He wants us to grow through it."

 # VIDEO TEACHING

Watch the Week 1 video teaching on your *Life Choices* Resource DVD.

MESSAGE NOTES

Below are the message notes included in the Student Guide. The fill-in answers are underlined and highlighted. The answers will also be displayed in text during the video teaching.

MESSAGE NOTES ANSWERS

1) To whom was James writing this letter? *__The Israelite people who had fled their homes__*.

2) In this passage, "consider" means to *__give this serious thought.__*

3) Joy is a *__choice__* while happiness is a *__feeling.__*

4) It's not *__if__* you will face trials, it's *__when__* you will face trials.

5) God tells us to be joyful when we're *__in the middle__* of trials, not when the trials are *__over__*.

6) When we choose *__joy__* in our trials, we come out of them looking more like *__Jesus__*.

7) When we don't have the strength to make the right choice, that's when we need *__each other__*.

ADDITIONAL QUESTIONS:

If you have more time available for small group discussion, use these Bible verses and questions.

> READ JAMES 1:2–4.

12. In the lesson, you heard that God sometimes uses trials to mature us and make us stronger. Have you found this to be true in your life? Share an example with your group.

13. Look at the issues you marked on the "My Life" page. Choose one of them and think about what might be different if you deliberately chose to view the issue with joy. Share your thoughts with the group.

 # LIFE CHOICES CHALLENGE

Read this challenge to your students and encourage them to complete the challenge sometime this week.

This week's challenge: *Think of one person you know who is going through tough stuff in their life and encourage them. Encourage them in the way you would want someone to encourage you.*

Ask your group members for prayer requests, then close your group meeting with prayer.

Notes

DAY 2

RELAX Take a moment to identify the distractions in your head. Take a deep breath. Ask God to help you hear His voice.

READ

> **Proverbs 24:10, 10:9, 11:27, 13:20, 14:14, 20:22**
> **Author: Solomon**
>
> *As you read these passages, underline in your Bible any words or phrases that stand out to you.*

REACT

In a sentence or two, summarize what these verses tell you.

What stands out to you from these verses? Why do you think it stands out?

NOTE: Solomon was a guy who seemingly had everything going for him, and yet in the Bible (in Ecclesiastes), he shares how even he struggled with despair. The truth is that we never really "graduate" from pain. Instead, like Solomon, we need to learn how to be strengthened by it.

How have you seen these verses to be true in your life? Be specific.

_____

_____

_____

RELATE:

In what specific way could you apply at least one of these verses to your life? (Proverbs 24:10, 10:9, 11:27, 13:20, 14:14, 20:22)

RESPOND:

Spend some time thanking God for these truths you read today. Confess to Him the times in your past when you have not lived out these truths. Ask God for strength to actually do what you feel challenged to do from the verses.

31

DAY 3

RELAX Clear the distractions from your head. Close your eyes and imagine God waiting to have a conversation with you.

READ

Job 1:13–22   Author: Unknown

As you read this passage, underline in your Bible any words or phrases that stand out to you.

REACT

In a sentence or two, summarize what this verse tells you.

"The Lord gave and the Lord has taken away, may the name of the Lord be praised." (v. 21) What do you think Job's prayer means?

NOTE: It can be easy to let our expectations (what we hope for) turn into a feeling of entitlement (thinking we deserve something). When that happens, it's easy to view trials as God letting us down. Instead, we need to let our expectations stay just what they are...expectations. Then when bad stuff happens, we don't blame God, because we were never promised a perfect life to begin with. Plus, we become extremely grateful when God brings us blessings of any kind.

Reread verses 21–22. When your life gets difficult, do you find yourself responding like Job? If not, how do you normally respond? Why do you think you respond that way?

Why do you think God included the story of Job in the Bible?

RELATE:

Step into the story for a moment and write down how you would feel if you were Job. (Job 1:13-22)

Now think of a difficult day either from your past or that you are dealing with presently—can you pray Job's prayer for yourself? Do it.

RESPOND:

Spend some time thanking God for Job's example. Tell God about the times when it's especially hard for you to respond well to trials. Ask Him for strength to do what you feel challenged to do from the story.

DAY 4

RELAX Take a few moments to identify what's distracting you. Ask God to turn down the volume of these distractions in your mind, so that you can hear His whisper as He speaks to you.

READ

> **John 11:1–44**
> **Author: Apostle John** *(one of Jesus' 12 Apostles)*
>
> *As you read this passage, underline in your Bible any words or phrases that stand out to you.*

REACT

In a sentence or two, summarize what these verses tell you.

What does this story teach you about God?

NOTE: Notice that Jesus knew from the beginning that He was going to raise Lazarus from the dead, yet in verse 35 we read that "Jesus wept." Even though God can see the big picture and knows that all things work for the good of those who love him (Romans 8:28), He still hurts with us while we are in the middle of our pain. Even in our toughest moments, we are truly never alone.

RELATE:

Step into the story for a moment and write down how you would feel if you were Mary or Martha. (John 11:1-44)

Now think of a struggle you're currently facing—what do you now know is true about God's involvement in your life based on the passage you read today?

RESPOND:

Thank God for this story and that He loves bringing people, families, dreams, and friendships from death to life. Confess times when you have doubted that God was really at work in your pain. Ask Him for strength to actually do what you feel challenged to do from the story.

DAY 5

READ

2 Corinthians 4   Author: Apostle Paul

As you read this passage, underline in your Bible any words or phrases that stand out to you.

REACT

In a sentence or two, summarize what these verses tell you.

_____

_____

What does this chapter teach you about God?

_____

_____

NOTE: Paul is, perhaps, the most famous Christian in history, yet in his letters he shared that he was constantly enduring trials. I heard a pastor one time state, "The amount of ministry God is able to give you is directly related to the amount of pain you are willing to endure." That was certainly true of Paul; he faced prison, beatings, shipwrecks, and rejection while helping firmly establish the Christian church.

Paul doesn't promise that we won't have trials sometimes (actually, he says the opposite), but he does promise us something else. What is it?

RELATE:

Make a list of the current trials in your life. Now make a list of the ways you can see God renewing you day by day *(e.g., hope, encouragement, purpose, conversation with a friend, small group, etc.).* (2 Corinthians 4)

Trial	God's Renewal

RESPOND:

Ask God to help you "fix your eyes" on the second list—on how He is renewing you in your life. Thank Him for the second list. Ask Him for strength to be able to actually do what you feel challenged to do from the passage.

DAY 6

RELAX Take a moment to identify the distractions in your head. Take a deep breath. Ask God to help you hear His voice.

READ

Matthew 26:36–46   Author: Apostle Matthew

As you read this passage, underline in your Bible any words or phrases that stand out to you.

REACT

What stands out to you from this story?

_____

_____

_____

What does this scene teach you about God?

_____

_____

NOTE: I've visited the Garden of Gethsemane, and while there I was struck by its perfect view of the city of Jerusalem. While praying in this hillside garden, Jesus was more than aware of what was coming the next day, yet He didn't run from it. Sometimes, the trials in our life are more than God wanting to do something in us—instead they are God wanting to do something **through** us.

How does it make you feel, knowing that we have a God who truly understands what it's like to be stressed out and feel alone?

RELATE:

Step into the story for a moment and imagine what it must have been like for Jesus, in His worst moments, to see His friends repeatedly fail him. Do you know anyone who might be feeling the same way? What can you do to let them know they are not alone...today? (Matthew 26:36–46)

RESPOND:

Spend some time thanking God for understanding our loneliness and pain. Tell Him about the times when you have "fallen asleep" when others really needed you, and ask for forgiveness. Ask Him for strength to be able to actually do what you feel challenged to do from the story.

39

DAY 7

RELAX Clear the distractions from your head. Close your eyes and imagine God waiting to have a conversation with you.

READ

Psalm 42   Author: David

As you read this passage, underline in your Bible any words or phrases that stand out to you.

Rewrite the psalm in your own words, verse by verse. When you finish, read your prayer out loud to God.

Verse 1

Verse 2

Verse 3

Verse 4

Verse 5

Verse 6

Verse 7

Verse 8

Verse 9

Verse 10

Verse 11

41

How have you lived out what you've learned from God this past week? Where did God show up in your life? Tell at least one story of what God taught you this week through your devotionals, or what happened when you applied what you're learning.

_____

_____

_____

_____

_____

How can you shine with God's light by challenging, encouraging, or inspiring the rest of your group with what God is teaching you? What things are you learning that you hope others in your group are learning, too? What things do you think they most need to know? What could you do together as a group to live out what God is teaching you?

199

_____

_____

_____

_____

_____

_____

FAMILY ISSUES

FAMILY ISSUES
GROUP MEETING

OPEN YOUR GROUP MEETING WITH PRAYER.

WEEKLY SCENARIO

*"A friend invited me to church about six months ago,
and I heard about Jesus for the first time. I'm not
exaggerating when I say He is the best thing that has
ever happened to me. I love my new brothers and sisters
and can't wait for Sunday mornings and Tuesday nights.
The only problem is that my parents definitely don't share
my same beliefs. They think God and church are getting
in the way of my studies (they aren't, by the way) and
have pretty much restricted me from going except during
vacation. I snuck out one time and I'm still hearing from
my parents about how I'm a hypocrite. I know the Bible
says to honor your parents, but what should I do?"*

🎞 MOVIE TIME

Watch the Week 2 movie clip on your *Life Choices* **Resource DVD.**

I'M DONE WITH YOU!

In this clip, Jake's mother leaves their home, and Jake confronts his father over his behavior.

"You're unbelievable,
you know that? I'm
done with you!"
— Jake to his father in *To Save A Life*

Ask the group to respond to the movie clip by volunteering to answer the questions below.

- What stood out to you in this movie clip? Was there anything you learned?

- Is there anything in this clip that applies to your life?

DISCUSSION QUESTIONS

Open the discussion by saying, "Tonight we are going to talk about three tough issues that affect families. The first one we'll tackle is *conflict*."

1. In 30 seconds or less, tell us about your family. (Go around the group and give each student an opportunity to share.)

2. When it comes to fighting, what is your family like? Rate your family on a scale of 1 to 10, where a "1" means life with your family is "a big giant tea party," and a "10" means it's more like a World Wrestling Entertainment smackdown. Explain your rating.

3. What issues cause the most arguments in your family? Why do you think that is?

4. Which of the following fighting methods do you normally use with members in your family? (Leader: Read the five options to your group.)
   - **I leave.** I don't want to fight, so I physically leave the room or I emotionally leave by refusing to participate in the argument.

45

- **I let the other person win.** Keeping the peace is so important that I agree to what the other person wants.

- **I give a little to get a little.** I give in to part of what the other person wants, so I can have part of what I want.

- **I look out for myself.** I do whatever is necessary to make sure I win the argument, even if it means the other person ends up hurt or angry with me.

- **I look out for the other person.** It's important that we both get what we want and need, so I try to work together with the other person to make it happen.

READ PHILIPPIANS 2:3-4 AND MATTHEW 7:3-5.

5. Of the five fighting methods, which one is closest to the Bible's description of how we ought to fight?

READ ROMANS 12:18.

6. What do you think you should do if the other members in your family could care less about "living in peace with everyone"? If they don't follow God's commands, does that mean you don't have to either? What good does it do to keep God's commands when they won't?

7. What do you think "as far as it depends on you" means? What aspects of a fight depend on you? What aspects are beyond your control?

READ EPHESIANS 6:1-3.

8. What are the two commands this passage gives to kids? Obedience is an *action*; honor is an *attitude*. Explain the difference and give examples.

9. What does it look like to fulfill these commands when you're in the middle of an argument?

10. What does God promise us if we obey and honor our parents in the Lord?

VIDEO TEACHING

Watch the week 2 video teaching on your *Life Choices* **Resource DVD**.
Also watch the video "Heather's Story."

MESSAGE NOTES

Below are the message notes included in the Student Guide. The fill-in
answers are underlined and highlighted.

MESSAGE NOTES ANSWERS

1) If you are suffering the consequences of a divorce, remember:

- Seek *help*. Don't *suffer in silence*.

- Realize and accept that *it's not your fault*.

- God has given you the *power to forgive*.

2) If you are suffering the consequences of any type of abuse,
remember:

- Find someone to *talk to*.

- Take whatever steps are necessary to *protect yourself from
serious abuse*.

- Let go of any *guilty feelings*.

- See yourself the way *God sees you*.

- Run to *God*.

3) How can I help my hurting friend?

- Give *comfort* (2 Corinthians 1:3–4).

- *Defend* the weak (Psalm 82:3–4).

47

ADDITIONAL QUESTIONS:

RE-READ 2 CORINTHIANS 2:3-4.

11. How has divorce affected your life or the lives of the people you know? What would you say or do for a friend who was going through a divorce?

RE-READ PSALM 82:1-4.

12. What would you say or do for a friend who was experiencing abuse?

 # LIFE CHOICES CHALLENGE

Read this challenge to your students and encourage them to complete the challenge sometime this week.

This week's challenge: *Take a positive step to deal with an issue that your family is struggling with. If there are no current issues, then write a note to your parent(s) thanking them for being good parents.*

Ask your group members for prayer requests, then close your group meeting with prayer.

Notes

DAY 9

RELAX Clear the distractions from your head. Close your eyes and take a few deep breaths. Imagine God turning down the volume of these distractions for you, so you can hear what He has to say.

READ

Proverbs 11:29, 15:17, 20:29, 23:22
Author: Solomon

As you read these passages, underline in your Bible any words or phrases that stand out to you.

REACT

What stands out to you from these verses?

_____

_____

Why do you think God included these verses in the Bible?
What can they teach us?

_____

_____

_____

How have you seen these verses to be true in your life and family?
Be specific.

_____

_____

_____

NOTE: Best-selling author Chuck Swindoll once said, "Life is 10% what happens to you and 90% how you react to it." His observation is similar to the truth found in Proverbs 15:17. You can eat your instant noodles for the fourth time this week and be thankful you have food, or you can complain that your tri-tip steak is a little too well done. Which of these attitudes do you usually take with your family?

RELATE:

Write down at least one specific way you could apply one or more of these verses to your life. (Proverbs 11:29, 15:17, 20:29, 23:22)

RESPOND:

Spend some time thanking God for these truths you read today. Confess to Him the times in your past when you have not lived out these truths. Ask God for strength to actually do what you feel challenged to do from the verses.

DAY 10

READ

2 Samuel 13:1–22   Author: Unknown

As you read this passage, underline in your Bible any words or phrases that stand out to you.

REACT

What stands out to you from this story?

_____

_____

The word "dysfunctional" means to not function properly, and unfortunately, it's a word that can sometimes apply to families. Write down some of the ways in which the family in this passage is dysfunctional.

_____

_____

What do you think David and his children could have done to fix their dysfunctional relationships and restore health to their family?

_____

_____

NOTE: As you read through the Bible, you might notice that just about everyone had to deal with pain in their life. For example, King David (Amnon and Tamar's dad) was known as a man after God's own heart, yet look at how his kids turned out. In this family, one tragic mistake led to even more mistakes and family dysfunction. What do you think might have happened if one person in the family had just put their foot down and said, "Enough is enough"?

RELATE:

Think about the way your own family functions. What are some things you can proactively do to fix dysfunctions and help your family behave in a healthy way? (2 Samuel 13:1-22)

RESPOND:

Spend some time thanking God for the story you read today. Confess any way in which you have added to your own family's dysfunction. Ask God for strength to actually do what you feel challenged to do from reading this Bible story.

53

DAY 11

RELAX Take a few moments to identify what's distracting you. Ask God to turn down the volume of these distractions in your mind, so that you can hear His whisper as He speaks to you.

READ

> **Luke 2:41–52**
> **Author: Luke** *(physician, historian, and traveling companion of the Apostle Paul)*
>
> *As you read this passage, underline in your Bible any words or phrases that stand out to you.*

REACT

What stands out to you from the story?

_____

_____

Why do you think God included this story in the Bible? What can you learn from it?

_____

_____

_____

NOTE: This is the only story we have of Jesus' life between the time He was a baby until He was 30 and beginning His ministry. It's interesting that Luke, the author of this gospel, chose to include an account of Jesus at the age of 12. God often begins to reveal what your life is going to be about when you're just starting middle school.

In verse 51, how does Jesus respond to His parents? Remember that Jesus is the Son of God. What can you learn from His example?

_____

_____

According to verse 52, in what ways did Jesus mature? What would that look like in your life?

_____

_____

RELATE:

Think through some of the issues you've had with your parents lately. How would a 12-year-old Jesus respond to those same issues? Write down your thoughts and then follow His example.
(Luke 2:41-52)

RESPOND:

Spend some time thanking God for this story. Confess when you have not followed Jesus' example regarding obedience to your parents. Ask God for strength to actually do what you feel challenged to do from the story.

DAY 12

READ

Ephesians 5:22–6:3   Author: Apostle Paul

As you read this passage, underline in your Bible any words or phrases that stand out to you.

NOTE: In the city of Ephesus, women and children were seen as second- or even third-class citizens—almost as if they were slaves. Yet Paul gives specific instructions to husbands to love and protect their wives, and for fathers to care for their children. A famous preacher once told his wife that he had "led two-and-a-half people to Christ." His wife responded, "Oh, two adults and one child?" And the preacher said, "No, two kids and one adult." (The adults' lives were already half over.)

REACT

What are some of the important concepts this passage teaches us about marriage?

_____

_____

_____

What are some of the important concepts this passage teaches us about children and parents?

_____

_____

Why do you think God included this passage in the Bible? What can you learn from it?

_____

_____

RELATE:

Spend a little time thinking about your relationship with your parents, and then write down one way you can obey them (through your actions) and honor them (with your attitude) tomorrow. Get really practical with your application.

(Ephesians 5:22–6:3)

RESPOND:

Spend some time thanking God for this passage, which clearly shows that God has a heart for families. Confess any ways in which you have not been living out this passage and then ask God for forgiveness. Ask Him for strength to actually do what you feel challenged to do from the passage.

DAY 13

RELAX Take a moment to identify the distractions in your head. Take a deep breath. Ask God to help you hear His voice.

READ

Luke 15:11–32   Author: Luke

As you read these passages, underline in your Bible any words or phrases that stand out to you.

REACT

What stands out to you from this story?

NOTE: To the first century Jewish audience, this story would have been radical. Because sons typically did not inherit until their father passed away, the younger son's request was the equivalent of telling his dad, "I wish you were dead." Any Jewish father would have been disgraced by such a request and would actually have had the right to kill such a disrespectful son. Instead, this father does the exact opposite.

What's God saying about His relationship with us through this story? How should this lesson impact our relationships with family members who wrong us?

Which brother do you most relate with in the story? Why?

What if the younger brother had first been greeted by his angry brother instead of his loving father? The end of the story would have been drastically different, right? When people in your family make mistakes, are they most likely to encounter angry siblings or loving parents?

RELATE:

Step into the story for a moment and imagine what it must have been like for the younger son to come home after losing half of his dad's money. If you were in the son's position, how would you feel? What about if you were the older brother? How would you feel seeing your younger brother return? (Luke 15:11-32)

How can you be a giver of grace and forgiveness in your family? Write down one specific way.

RESPOND:

Make a list of things God has given you, for which you should be thankful. Confess the times when you have been more concerned with giving out justice to family members than giving out grace. Ask God for strength to actually do what you feel challenged to do from the story.

59

DAY 14

RELAX Clear the distractions from your head. Close your eyes and imagine God waiting to have a conversation with you.

READ

Psalm 68:1–10   Author: David

As you read this passage, underline in your Bible any words or phrases that stand out to you.

Rewrite the psalm in your own words, verse by verse. When you finish, read your prayer out loud to God.

Verse 1

Verse 2

Verse 3

Verse 4

Verse 5

Verse 6

Verse 7

Verse 8

Verse 9

Verse 10

How have you lived out what you've learned from God this past week? Where did God show up in your life? Tell at least one story of what God taught you this week through your devotionals, or what happened when you applied what you're learning.

_____

_____

_____

_____

_____

How can you shine with God's light by challenging, encouraging, or inspiring the rest of your group with what God is teaching you? What things are you learning that you hope others in your group are learning, too? What things do you think they most need to know? What could you do together as a group to live out what God is teaching you?

_____

_____

_____

_____

_____

_____

FRIEND ISSUES

PURPOSE

To demonstrate the impact friends can have on our actions and our faith, and to inspire teens to be a life-changing influence on their friends.

KEY SCRIPTURES

1 Corinthians 15:33

OPEN YOUR GROUP MEETING WITH PRAYER.

WEEKLY SCENARIO

"I'm a Christian, but several of my best friends are not. I really want them to have a relationship with Jesus, but they don't appear to be interested. My friends love to do stuff I know is against God's teachings, but I keep finding myself following along just so I can stay close with them. Each time I do, though, I have lots of regrets. But if I just ditch them, then I'll never get the chance to share my faith. What should I do?"

 # MOVIE TIME

Watch the Week 3 movie clip on your *Life Choices* **Resource DVD**.

BEER PONG
In this scene, Jake faces peer pressure to drink at a party and deals with the consequences when he chooses to walk away.

"Whatever, Jake Taylor never misses a party."
— Doug to Jake in To Save A Life

Ask the group to respond to the movie clip by volunteering to answer the questions below.

- What stood out to you in this movie clip? Was there anything you learned?

- Is there anything in this clip that applies to your life?

DISCUSSION QUESTIONS

1. What one thing really stood out to you from your study so far in the *Life Choices* **Student Guide?**

   Leader, share the following with your group:

   "We dealt with some pretty intense stuff last week, and I'd like to give you an opportunity to encourage each other or ask for help."

   Take a few moments to allow students to share their experiences, encouraging them to "show the love" to one another as group members appear vulnerable or transparent.

   Give everyone in the group a blank piece of paper and a pen/pencil. Ask them to take two to three minutes to draw a picture of themselves and their closest friend(s), depicting what they do for fun together, their different personalities, and who acts as a "leader" among them.

2. Explain your picture to the rest of the group. The rest of the group can ask questions if they would like any clarification.

3. Share an example of when one of your friends influenced you in a positive way, e.g., helped you learn or improve in a sport, invited you to church, etc. How have you influenced your friends in a positive way?

4. Share an example of when one of your friends influenced you in a negative way. How have you influenced a friend in a negative way?

   Leader, share the following with your group:

   "Tonight we're going to look at some examples of people in the Bible who influenced those around them."

READ LUKE 19:1-10.

65

5. What method does Jesus use to influence Zacchaeus? Note that people referred to Zacchaeus as a "sinner," but Jesus referred to him as "son of Abraham." How do other people's words affect how we act and live—especially words from people we respect?

READ MATTHEW 14:22-29.

6. What method does Jesus use to influence Peter and the rest of the disciples? How do our friends' actions affect how we act and live?

READ ACTS 9:1-6.

7. What method does Jesus use to influence Paul? What is difficult about challenging others' bad decisions? How would you approach a friend to prevent them from making a poor or dangerous choice?

Leader, share the following with your group:

 "For every one of these positive ways to influence people, there is an equally powerful negative method of influence. For example, you can discourage people using just your words, you can give others a bad example to follow, or you can stay quiet when you know someone is making a bad choice. But remember that you're not the only one with the ability to influence—every day, everyone around you is influencing you somehow, either positively or negatively. They are either drawing you closer to what God desires for you, or they are pulling you further away."

READ 1 CORINTHIANS 15:33 AND HEBREWS 10:24-25.

8. Do these verses mean people should only hang out with those who are a "good influence" on them (i.e., should Christians only hang out with other Christians)? Is this how Jesus lived? Give examples to support your answer.

🍎 VIDEO TEACHING

Watch the week 3 video teaching on your *Life Choices* Resource DVD.

MESSAGE NOTES

Below are the message notes included in the Student Guide. The fill-in answers are underlined and highlighted.

MESSAGE NOTE ANSWERS

1) They were **slow to learn**.

Ask yourself: Is my faith growing or stagnant?

2) They couldn't **teach others**.

Ask yourself: When do I bring up God in my conversations with non-Christian friends?

3) They were still **spiritual babies**.

Ask yourself: Does my "spiritual age" (the years I've been a Christian) match my spiritual maturity?

ADDITIONAL QUESTIONS:

9. How does your relationship with God affect how you are as a friend? How does your own spiritual maturity affect your ability to be a positive influence versus being negatively influenced?

10. How full is your "cup" right now? Is it overflowing, pretty full, half-full, a few last drops, or empty?

 # LIFE CHOICES CHALLENGE

Read this challenge to your students and encourage them to complete the challenge some time this week.

This week's challenge: *Approach someone who has been a really good influence in your life and thank them. If you can't think of someone, look for someone who might be a good influence on you and intentionally try to spend more time with them.*

Ask your group members for prayer requests, and then close your group meeting with prayer.

DAY 16

RELAX Take a moment to identify the distractions in your head. Take a deep breath. Ask God to help you hear His voice.

READ

Proverbs 16:28, 17:17, 18:24, 27:6
Author: Solomon

As you read these passages, underline in your Bible any words or phrases that stand out to you.

REACT

What stands out to you from these verses?

_____

_____

_____

NOTE: There are really two sides of love: grace and truth. Solomon talks about both of them. Sometimes, love means forgiving someone and helping them move on. Sometimes, love means getting in their face and telling them to stop messing around.

In what ways have you seen these verses to be true in your life?

Which friend (or friends) in your life demonstrates the truth of these verses? In what way?

RELATE:

How can you live out these verses and for which friend(s)? Be specific in your answer. (Proverbs 16:28, 17:17, 18:24, 27:6)

RESPOND:

Spend some time thanking God for these truths you read today. Confess to Him the times in your past when you have not lived out these truths. Ask God for strength to actually do what you feel challenged to do from the verses.

DAY 17

RELAX Clear the distractions from your head. Close your eyes and imagine God waiting to have a conversation with you.

READ

1 Samuel 20   Author: Solomon

As you read this passage, underline in your Bible any words or phrases that stand out to you.

REACT

What stands out to you from this story?

_____

_____

_____

_____

_____

_____

_____

NOTE: A number of Bible scholars believe that Jonathan was probably 25 years older than David. So, in terms of their age, they were not peers. Sometimes, the best friendships can be with people who are younger or older than you.

Step into the story for a moment and imagine that you're Jonathan. You're the heir to the throne, the second-most powerful person in the country, and yet God has picked David to be the next king. How do you think you would have reacted to David? What do you think makes Jonathan's friendship with David so incredible?

Scan through the chapter and pick the verse(s) you think provides the most inspiring example of true friendship. Why did you pick that specific verse(s)?

RELATE:

Do you have any relationships like this in your life—in which both of you care more about the other person and fulfilling God's plan than your own success? (1 Samuel 20)

If so, thank them and maybe even write a covenant together like in the story. If not, think about who might be that type of friend.

RESPOND:

Spend some time thanking God for these truths you read today. Confess the times when you have been a selfish friend who is more interested in your own success. Ask God for strength to be able to actually do what you feel challenged to do from the story.

71

DAY 18

READ

> **Mark 2:1–12**
> **Author: Mark** (traveling companion and close friend of the Apostle Peter)
>
> *As you read these passages, underline in your Bible any words or phrases that stand out to you.*

REACT

What stands out to you from this story?

_____

_____

_____

_____

NOTE: We never learn in the story if the man really wanted his friends to go to all this trouble or not. Maybe he was embarrassed or fearful. Maybe he was afraid the rope might snap and he would fall. Sometimes, being a great friend is doing what's right for someone even if they don't ask, or even agree with your actions.

Why was the man healed? According to Jesus, whose faith was a part of this miracle?

_____

_____

Why do you think these men were willing to go to such lengths to get their friend to Jesus?

_____

_____

RELATE:

How does this story inspire you to bring your friends to Jesus—even when you face what seems to be a dead end? (Mark 2:1-12)

_____

_____

What's one specific step of faith you could take that would help a friend get closer to Jesus?

_____

RESPOND:

Spend some time thanking God for these truths you read today. Confess to Him the times in your past when you have not lived out these truths. Ask God for strength to actually do what you feel challenged to do from the verses.

DAY 19

RELAX Clear the distractions from your head. Close your eyes and take a few deep breaths. Imagine God turning down the volume of these distractions for you, so you can hear what He has to say.

READ

2 Corinthians 1:3–11   Author: Apostle Paul

As you read this passage, underline in your Bible any words or phrases that stand out to you.

REACT

What stands out to you from this passage?

_____

_____

_____

_____

NOTE: In his letters, the Apostle Paul used the word "overflow" five times to describe how the Christian life is supposed to be lived out. That very descriptive word illustrates that it's not a case of us just trying harder and harder to be good Christians. Instead, we are to surrender everything to God and let Him overflow His love from our lives onto the people around us.

In verse 3, Paul describes God in two ways; what are they?

_____

_____

What are we supposed to do with the comfort and compassion we receive from God?

_____

_____

RELATE:

Make a list of several ways in which God has comforted you. (Remember that God can use people to provide us with comfort.)

_____

_____

_____

Now, make another list of two to three people to whom you could overflow some of God's comfort. Offer them comfort this week, or even today if you have the opportunity.

1) _____

2) _____

3) _____

RESPOND:

Spend some time thanking God for these truths you read today. Ask Him for strength to be able to actually overflow God's comfort and compassion onto the people around you.

DAY 20

RELAX Take a moment to identify the distractions in your head. Take a deep breath. Ask God to help you hear His voice.

READ

Matthew 13:1-17   Author: Apostle Matthew

As you read these passages, underline in your Bible any words or phrases that stand out to you.

REACT

What stands out to you from this story?

_____

_____

What does this story show you about how Jesus treated His friends?

_____

NOTE: They didn't have Nikes back in the first century; everyone wore sandals. Jesus and His disciples walked miles from town to town wearing open sandals, and they must have had really grimy feet. Given how dirty people's feet became after walking on the dirt roads, foot washing was viewed as a job fit only for a slave. And sometimes, it was considered even below a slave's dignity!

On the night described in this passage, Jesus already knew that two of His friends would betray Him (Judas) and deny Him (Peter), yet Jesus took on the job normally given to a slave and washed their feet. What does Jesus' action say about how we should treat our friends?

RELATE:

Step into the story for a moment and imagine being one of the disciples having their feet washed by Jesus. What would you be thinking and feeling? (Matthew 13:1-17)

Write down at least one specific, loving, and almost irrational way you can serve the people closest to you this week.

1)

2)

RESPOND:

Spend some time thanking God for these truths you read today. Confess where you have not gone out of your way to serve others this past week. Ask God for strength to live out this story in your own world in the week to come.

DAY 21

RELAX Clear the distractions from your head. Close your eyes and imagine God waiting to have a conversation with you.

READ

Psalm 23   Author: David

As you read this passage, underline in your Bible any words or phrases that stand out to you.

Rewrite the psalm in your own words, verse by verse. When you finish, read your prayer out loud to God.

Verse 1

Verse 2

Verse 3

Verse 4

Verse 5

Verse 6

How have you lived out what you've learned from God this past week? Where did God show up in your life? Tell at least one story of what God taught you this week through your devotionals, or what happened when you applied what you're learning.

_____

_____

_____

_____

_____

How can you shine with God's light by challenging, encouraging, or inspiring the rest of your group with what God is teaching you? What things are you learning that you hope others in your group are learning, too? What things do you think they most need to know? What could you do together as a group to live out what God is teaching you?

_____

_____

_____

_____

_____

_____

SEX AND DATING ISSUES

SEX AND DATING ISSUES
GROUP MEETING

PURPOSE
To help students understand that God created sex and clearly reserved it for the committed, loving, and intimate context of marriage.

KEY SCRIPTURES
Genesis 2:24–25; Song of Solomon 7:1–9; Ephesians 5:25–32
1 Corinthians 6:18–20; Philippians 2:14–15

OPEN YOUR GROUP MEETING WITH PRAYER.

WEEKLY SCENARIO

"I'm 17, and I've been dating a guy I really like for almost nine months now. We're both wearing purity rings, and we even talked about setting boundaries on our physical relationship. But it just seems like our relationship is too intense. We spend almost all our free time together, and we talk about stuff that we've never shared with anyone else. Although we haven't crossed any physical lines yet, it's slowly moving in that direction. Other than not having sex, it almost seems like we're married. I've mentioned this to my boyfriend, but he doesn't think it's a big deal. I mean, we love each other, and that's what's important... isn't it? What should I do?"

🎞️ MOVIE TIME

Watch the Week 4 movie clip on your *Life Choices* **Resource DVD.**

AMY'S PREGNANT

In this scene, Amy tells Jake she's pregnant and he's the father. Jake's response and his attempts to help just make the issue worse.

"great, make me feel worse than I already do!"
— *Amy to Jake in To Save A Life*

Ask the group to respond to the movie clip by volunteering to answer the questions below.

- What stood out to you in this movie clip? Was there anything you learned?

- Is there anything in this clip that applies to your life?

🍎 VIDEO TEACHING

Watch the first part of the Week 4 video teaching on your *Life Choices* **Resource DVD.**

MESSAGE NOTES

Below are the message notes included in the Student Guide. The fill-in answers are underlined.

> ## MESSAGE NOTE ANSWERS
>
> 1) God created ___*sex*___ and ___*pleasure*___.
>
> 2) Satan is in the business of ___*distorting sex*___ and ___*stealing pleasure*___.
>
> 3) God invented marriage and sex to give us a glimpse of how much He ___*loves us*___.

DISCUSSION QUESTIONS

1. What do you think about what we just heard? Is there anything with which you particularly agree or disagree? If so, why?

   Leader, share the following with your group:

   "Before we go on with more questions, I want to give you total freedom to share whatever you're feeling right now. This group is a safe place, and I must remind you all of the house rules. Whatever is shared in this group will not leave the group. OK?"

   Make sure all students respond verbally or visually that they agree.

   Wait a few moments, and if nobody shares, move forward with the rest of the questions. If people do begin to share, skip some or all of the remaining questions as time requires (and PRAY HARD for God to bless this time of sharing!).

2. Based on what we just heard, why do you think sex is such a huge issue to God?

3. Read the following verses and discuss what each passage teaches about sex.
   - Genesis 2:21–25
   - Ephesians 5:3
   - Philippians 4:8–9
   - Matthew 5:27–30
   - 1 Corinthians 6:18–20
   - 1 John 1:9

   Give everyone in your group a blank piece of paper (or have them turn to a page in their Student Guide that has some

Note to the Reader

There are a few corrections to this guide:

1. Page 34: While many of the Psalms were written by King David, the author of Psalm 42 is unknown.

2. Page 58: The author of 1 Samuel is unknown.

3. Pages 60 and 61: Mark 2:1-12 does tell the story of Jesus healing the paralytic, but the version recorded in Luke

Note to the Reader

There are a few corrections to this guide:

1. Page 40: While many of the Psalms were written by King David, the author of Psalm 42 is unknown.

2. Page 70: The author of 1 Samuel is unknown.

3. Pages 72 and 73: Mark 2:1-12 does tell the story of Jesus healing the paralytic, but the version recorded in Luke 5:17-26 will provide you with more detailed tion in the Day 18 study. We

recommend that you read both Scriptures, or read
Luke 5:17-26 only.

4. Pages 76 and 77: The Scripture reference should
be John 13:1-17, rather than Matthew 13:1-17. The
author of this Scripture is the Apostle John.

Please accept our apologies for these errors and any
inconvenience they might cause during your study. We will
correct the errors in future versions of this guide.

questions in the Day 18 study. We recommend that you read both Scriptures, or read Luke 5:17-26 only.

4. Pages 64 and 65: The Scripture reference should be John 13:1-17, rather than Matthew 13:1-17. The author of this Scripture is the Apostle John.

Please accept our apologies for these errors and any inconvenience they might cause during your study. We will correct the errors in future versions of this guide.

blank space) and write a letter to God, confessing any of the areas in which they have misused sex. Remind students that their letters are strictly between them and God; they will not be asked to share their letter.

4. What do you need to do to make sure you don't fall into some of these same traps again? Be as practical as you can (e.g., "Actually write out sexual boundaries for a relationship," "Be picky about who I date," etc.).

Continued
VIDEO TEACHING

Watch the second part of the Week 4 video teaching on your *Life Choices* **Resource DVD.**

MESSAGE NOTES *(CONTINUED)*

Below is the fourth message note in the Student Guide. The fill-in answer is underlined and highlighted.

MESSAGE NOTE ANSWER

4) Sexual purity is not a ***line you cross*** but a ***lifestyle you live.***

⚠ LIFE CHOICES CHALLENGE

Read this challenge to your students and encourage them to complete the challenge sometime this week.

This week's challenge: *Give up television, texting, Internet, or music for the rest of the week.*

Ask your group members for prayer requests, then close your group meeting with prayer.

DAY 23

RELAX Clear the distractions from your head. Close your eyes and take a few deep breaths. Imagine God turning down the volume of these distractions for you, so you can hear what He has to say.

READ

Proverbs 7   Author: Solomon

As you read this passage, underline in your Bible any words or phrases that stand out to you.

REACT

What stands out to you from this story?

NOTE: Solomon is also the author of the Song of Solomon, which is easily the most sexually oriented book in the Bible. He clearly sees a difference between sex outside of marriage and sex with the person to whom you've committed the rest of your life.

In verses 22–23, Solomon describes this young man's decision using harsh visual images. Why do you think he used this literary technique?

In verses 1 and 2, Solomon makes it clear that the reader should pay attention to his words. Why do you think people sometimes ignore advice, particularly when it comes from someone older and more experienced?

RELATE:

Verse 25 says, "Don't let your heart turn to her ways…" How do you think your heart could "turn" to someone's "ways"? What are the sexual temptations you face in your life? (Proverbs 7)

RESPOND:

Thank God for the wisdom in this passage. Confess any ways in which you have fallen for sexual temptations. Thank God that He always forgives us after we confess our sins. Pray that this young man's story will not be your story.

DAY 24

RELAX Take a moment to identify the distractions in your head. Take a deep breath. Ask God to help you hear His voice.

READ

2 Samuel 11   Author: Unknown

As you read this passage, underline in your Bible any words or phrases that stand out to you.

REACT

What stands out to you from this story?

Make a list of all the bad decisions David made in this passage. What can you learn from this list?

What do you think would have happened if David had been honest at any point in the story?

_____

_____

NOTE: After David marries Bathsheba, God sends a prophet to confront him over his sins. Later this week, you will read Psalm 51, in which David repents of his sins before God. Sin doesn't just hurt people; it truly hurts our relationship with God.

RELATE:

Step into the story for a moment. Why do you think David kept making stupid decisions? (2 Samuel 11)

What does poor decision-making look like in your own life in terms of sexual purity, dating, and the opposite sex? Be specific in your answer.

RESPOND:

Thank God for the wisdom in this passage. Confess to God any ways in which you covered up for past mistakes instead of being honest with the people you wronged and with God. Thank God that He always forgives us after we confess our sins. Pray that God will show you how you can apply this new wisdom to your life.

DAY 25

RELAX Take a few moments to identify what's distracting you. Ask God to turn down the volume of these distractions in your mind, so that you can hear His whisper as He speaks to you.

READ

Hebrews 13:1-6   Author: Unknown

As you read this passage, underline in your Bible any words or phrases that stand out to you.

REACT

What stands out to you from this passage?

_____

_____

This passage deals with a whole range of topics. List the topics below. What do you think they all have in common?

_____

_____

NOTE: The book of Hebrews shares in detail what God has done for us through His love and grace. In the last chapter of Hebrews, the author writes that we should respond to God's gifts by loving each other. Staying pure is not just a good thing to do—it should be our response to Christ dying on the cross for our sins.

Notice that many of the sentences start with words or phrases like, "Keep on...," "Do not forget...," "Remember...." These were not new instructions from the author; he wanted to remind his readers of them over and over again. What specifically can you do to "not forget" the things you've been learning, but rather live them out?

The passage says, "God will judge the adulterer and all the sexually immoral." Why do you think He's so strict with sexual sins?

RELATE:

What are the temptations in your life that might prevent you from keeping your (future) marriage bed pure? How can you avoid or resist these temptations?

RESPOND:

Thank God for the teaching in this passage and for His message of grace. Confess to Him the times when you have not loved others. Thank God for His promise that He will never leave you nor forsake you.

DAY 26

RELAX Clear the distractions from your head. Close your eyes and take a few deep breaths. Imagine God turning down the volume of these distractions for you, so you can hear what He has to say.

READ

1 Corinthians 6:12–18   Author: Apostle Paul

As you read this passage, underline in your Bible any words or phrases that stand out to you.

REACT

What stands out to you from this passage?

_____

_____

_____

NOTE: Today's passage implies that sexual immorality is a unique type of sin, and possibly even a bigger issue than other sins. Consider the reference in verse 16 to becoming "one flesh." Everywhere else in the Bible, the term "one flesh" is used to refer to the committed, intimate, and trusting relationship between a husband and wife. Think of sex outside marriage as your body becoming one flesh—in a physically, emotionally, and spiritually intimate manner—with someone to whom you don't belong. No wonder Paul refers to it as a sin against the body!

According to this passage, why is sexual immorality such a big deal to God?

_____

_____

What are practical, specific ways in which you can "flee" from sexual immorality *(see verse 18)*?

_____

_____

RELATE:

Paul says that our bodies are actually members of Christ. According to that, your eyes, ears, mouth, and sexual organs actually belong to God. In what ways do you cause Christ to do things He doesn't want to do? *(For example: Do you cause His eyes to see movies He doesn't want to see?)* (1 Corinthians 6:12-18)

RESPOND:

Thank God for speaking to you today. Confess to Him the times in your past when you have misused parts of the body that He has given you. Thank God that He always forgives us after we confess our sins.

93

DAY 27

RELAX Take a moment to identify the distractions in your head. Take a deep breath. Ask God to help you hear His voice.

READ

John 8:1–11   Author: Apostle John

As you read this passage, underline in your Bible any words or phrases that stand out to you.

REACT

What stands out to you from this story?

_____

_____

Notice what Jesus does when the people throw the woman at his feet (verse 8b). How might that have been significant to her in that moment?

_____

_____

NOTE: Adultery requires two people, and yet only the woman is brought before Jesus. In the first century Jewish culture, women were seen as second-class citizens with fewer rights than men. But notice Jesus' reaction to this woman. This is one of many stories in the New Testament where Jesus treats men and women with equality.

What does this story teach you if you've made sexual mistakes in the past? What does it teach you about how you should treat others who are struggling with sexual sins?

Does this passage demonstrate that Jesus approves of sexual immorality? Why or why not?

RELATE:

Step into the story for a moment. Where can you see yourself in this story? Are you the woman? Someone holding a stone? Jesus?

(John 8:1-11)

Grab a rock from outside and write the word "forgiven" on it. Carry it around for a while and explain to people what it means to you.

RESPOND:

Thank God for the wisdom in this passage. If you identify with the woman in the story, then pray for strength to leave your life of sin. Ask God to give you an opportunity this week to show His grace to someone.

95

DAY 28

RELAX Clear the distractions from your head. Close your eyes and imagine God waiting to have a conversation with you.

READ

Psalm 51:1–12   Author: David

As you read this passage, underline in your Bible any words or phrases that stand out to you.

Rewrite the psalm in your own words, verse by verse. When you finish, read your prayer out loud to God.

Verse 1

Verse 2

Verse 3

Verse 4

Verse 5

Verse 6

Verse 7

Verse 8

Verse 9

Verse 10

Verse 11

Verse 12

How have you lived out what you've learned from God this past week? Where did God show up in your life? Tell at least one story of what God taught you this week through your devotionals, or what happened when you applied what you're learning.

_____

_____

_____

_____

_____

How can you shine with God's light by challenging, encouraging, or inspiring the rest of your group with what God is teaching you? What things are you learning that you hope others in your group are learning, too? What things do you think they most need to know? What could you do together as a group to live out what God is teaching you?

_____

_____

_____

_____

_____

_____

_____

GOD ISSUES

GOD ISSUES

PURPOSE

To help students identify where they are in their spiritual journey, and then encourage them to bear fruit through a committed and constantly growing relationship with Christ.

KEY SCRIPTURES

Matthew 13:1–9 & 18–23; and Colossians 3:17

OPEN YOUR GROUP MEETING WITH PRAYER.

WEEKLY SCENARIO

"Two years ago, I went to summer retreat with a church. At the end of the retreat, they asked if anyone wanted to make a decision for Christ, and I stepped forward. It felt really good at the time, but after I got home from the retreat, I just seemed to get caught up in my normal routine of school, hanging out with friends, soccer practice, and all that stuff. I haven't read my Bible in months. Now, I feel guilty about it and I'm not sure what happened."

🎞 MOVIE TIME

Watch the Week 5 movie clip on your *Life Choices* **Resource DVD**.

ON HIS KNEES
In this scene, Jake gets down on his knees in his bedroom to pray to God for help.

"Umm, god, I don't know if I'm allowed to be mad at you, but I am."
–Jake to God in To Save A Life

Ask the group to respond to the movie clip by volunteering to answer the questions below.

- What stood out to you in this movie clip? Was there anything you learned?

- Is there anything in this clip that applies to your life?

SPIRITUAL TRUE OR FALSE

This week includes an extra activity for your group. Explain to the students that you are going to read some statements. After each statement, they should indicate whether the statement is true or false for them. You can go around the group and ask each person, or you can have them answer by raising their hand when you say "True" or "False."

Statements:

- I think about spiritual stuff a lot.

- My family often talks about God.

- I've known someone who claimed to be a "Christian" but didn't live it out.

- I sometimes have doubts about my faith.

- The Bible is easy for me to understand.

- I sometimes feel guilty that I don't "do enough" for God.

– I have a hard time paying attention when I pray.

– I feel closer to God than I did a year ago.

– I sometimes wonder if I am really going to heaven after I die.

DISCUSSION QUESTIONS

1. Which of the True and False statements really stood out to you and why?

2. Were you at all surprised by other people's answers? Why or why not?

3. At the end of the movie *To Save A Life*, Chris says, "Faith is a journey. The journey is not so much about a destination but a transformation." What do you think that means? Do you agree with him?

4. If someone said to you that the two most important questions you need to answer in your life are, "Is there a God and if so, what does He want with me?" would you agree with that statement? Why or why not?

Leader, share the following with your group:

Our ministry is really about helping people find answers to those two questions. So, in the next few minutes, we're going to read and discuss a parable that might help you identify where you are in your spiritual journey."

READ MATTHEW 13:1-9.

5. What do you think this parable means?

Leader, once the group has had a chance to discuss the parable, have a student read Matthew 13:18–23. Then share the following:

"Using this parable, let's unpack each of these four ways people respond to God."

OPTION 1: *THE PATH* REPRESENTS THOSE WHO ARE NOT INTERESTED.

6. Why do you think some people are just not interested in hearing about Jesus? What are some of the possible reasons?

From what you know of Jesus, does He ever force people who are not interested to be interested? Does Jesus ever seem to get mad at those who don't believe? Do you think the path is where Jesus wants us to be?

OPTION 2: *THE ROCKS* REPRESENT THOSE WHOSE FAITH IS TOO SHALLOW.

7. Some people hear what God has done for them and eagerly accept His free gift of dying on the cross for their sins. But for some reason their faith just doesn't last, and they revert to their life before God. Why do you think some people respond to God and then let their faith die out? Does Jesus try to make these people feel guilty so they will follow Him again? Does Jesus say the plants that wither won't eventually grow back and be healthy? From what you know about this passage, is this where Jesus wants us to be?

OPTION 3: *THE THORNS* REPRESENT THOSE WHO ARE TOO BUSY.

8. Some people hear what God has done for them, excitedly accept His free gift of salvation and, though they never intentionally turn away from Him, their lives get busy and the busyness crowds out God. What are possible reasons that some people allow their lives to get so busy that they actually choke out God? From what you know about this passage, is this where Jesus wants us to be?

OPTION 4: *THE GOOD SOIL* REPRESENTS THOSE WHO ARE FRUITFUL.

9. Some people hear what God has done for them, excitedly accept His free gift and then just can't keep that gift to themselves; they share it with others. Based on Matthew 13:1–9, how can we know we're on the good soil? From what you know about this passage, is this where Jesus wants us to be?

OPTION 5: *NEVER HEARD*

Leader, share the following with your group:

"Let me give a fifth option: <u>Never Heard.</u> This means no one has really ever explained to you how to have a relationship with God."

10. Which of these five options best describes your faith right now? Not interested? Too shallow? Too busy? Fruitful? Give specific reasons why you chose a certain option.

Leader, if someone in your group identifies themselves with the fifth option, immediately ask if they would like to hear how they can have a relationship with God. If they agree, then walk them through a presentation of the Gospel. If they accept Christ, then encourage the group to celebrate.

VIDEO TEACHING

Watch the Week 5 video teaching on your *Life Choices* Resource DVD.

MESSAGE NOTES

Below are the message notes included in the Student Guide. The fill-in answers are underlined and highlighted.

MESSAGE NOTE ANSWERS

1) If you're on the rocks: God won't become *real to you* until you stop thinking of Him as a *concept* and start experiencing Him *personally*.

2) If you're on the rocks or the thorns: A relationship with God will never be all that it could be if you settle for *TV dinner* instead of *chicken pot pie*.

3) If you're on the good soil: At any given point in your life there are probably *one or two people* God wants you to deliberately *pour your life into*.

4) Which soil are you? _____

5) What are you going to do about it?_____

ADDITIONAL QUESTIONS:

Leader, share the following with your group:

"Here's a scary thought. The rocks, thorns, and good soil all appear to respond to Jesus in the same way at first. They each are excited at first, but then only the good soil stays strong and lives out a life that influences other people for Christ. A recent study reported that 88% of teenagers involved in a high school youth group are no longer going to church a year after graduation. In the coming years, there will be huge opportunities for you to settle for being in with the rocks or the thorns."

1. What do you think are the most important things you need to do to make sure you stay on the good soil?

2. Take it one step further…what are you going to do? Write down some specific steps.

 # LIFE CHOICES CHALLENGE

Read this challenge to your students and encourage them to complete the challenge sometime this week.

This week's challenge: *Write up your own challenge and exchange it with someone else.*

Ask your group members for prayer requests, then close your group meeting with prayer.

DAY 30

RELAX Take a moment to identify the distractions in your head. Take a deep breath. Ask God to help you hear His voice.

READ

Proverbs 3:5–6, Proverbs 16:1–9   Author: Solomon

As you read these passages, underline in your Bible any words or phrases that stand out to you.

REACT

What stands out to you from these verses?

_____

_____

_____

_____

What can you learn about God from these verses?

_____

_____

_____

_____

The Bible includes a number of verses about God guiding our steps (e.g., Psalm 37:23, Proverbs 4:12 and 20:24). In what ways have you seen God guide your steps?

_____

_____

_____

NOTE: In Proverbs 3:5-6, notice the use of the small but very powerful word ALL. Solomon learned that we don't just need to trust God for the big decisions or in big moments—we need to trust God in <u>every</u> decision, <u>every</u> day of our lives. When you start doing that, He will make your paths straight.

RELATE:

What is one specific way you could apply at least one of these verses to your life? (Proverbs 3:5-6, Proverbs 16:1-9)

RESPOND:

Spend some time thanking God for these truths you read today. Confess to Him the times in your past when you have not lived out these truths. Ask God for strength to actually do what you feel challenged to do from the verses.

107

DAY 31

RELAX Clear the distractions from your head. Close your eyes and imagine God waiting to have a conversation with you.

READ

Genesis 3   Author: Moses

As you read this passage, underline in your Bible any words or phrases that stand out to you.

REACT

What stands out to you from this story?

_____

_____

_____

In what ways does the serpent tempt Adam and Eve? Write down some of the methods you see him use in this passage.

_____

_____

_____

NOTE: Notice how Adam and Eve responded when they were caught in sin: First, they attempted to hide, then they tried to blame someone else. Adam blamed Eve and Eve pointed a blaming finger at the serpent. Adam even tried to assign some of the responsibility to God ("the woman You put here with me…"). Unfortunately, hiding and casting blame are all-too-common responses to the guilt that comes from sin.

Today, how do we still hide and blame after we've sinned?

RELATE:

Step into the story for a moment. Imagine you're at the tree; what would the serpent use to tempt you? Why do you think you're vulnerable to that type of "bait"? (Genesis 3)

In what ways have you hidden (been fearful of showing your real self) or blamed others for your mistakes?

RESPOND:

Spend some time thanking God for these truths you read today. Confess to Him the times in your past when you have hidden or blamed others, like Adam and Eve. Ask God for strength to trust Him instead of giving in to the temptations you face.

109

DAY 32

RELAX Take a few moments to identify what's distracting you. Ask God to turn down the volume of these distractions in your mind, so that you can hear His whisper as He speaks to you.

READ

Luke 18:18–30   Author: Luke

As you read this passage, underline in your Bible any words or phrases that stand out to you.

REACT

What stands out to you from this story?

_____

_____

In verse 20, Jesus refers to a well-known passage from the Old Testament. Do you recognize it? What is it?

_____

_____

NOTE: Jesus didn't just want this man's obedience; He wanted his heart. Through His questions, Jesus exposed the fact that this young ruler's heart was more connected to his money than it was to following God. The man needed to trust God instead of trusting in his own righteousness.

This man's stumbling block to God was his wealth; what might yours be? (For example, is yours good looks, popularity, sports, another relationship, etc.?)

_____

_____

In the story, even if the man would have given all his wealth away to the poor, he still would have not been good enough to inherit eternal life on his own merits. What was wrong with the man's question (and the answer he expected)?

_____

_____

RELATE:

Step into the story for a moment. If you were interested in knowing how to receive eternal life, what question would you have asked? From what you know about the Gospel, what would Jesus' answer have been? (Luke 18:18-30)

RESPOND:

Jesus was making the point that we can't DO enough to earn eternal life. We fall dreadfully short (like the rich young ruler). The great news of Jesus is that He died to make up the difference for where we fall short. Take some time thanking God in prayer for the powerful truth that no matter what we've done or not done, through God's grace we can be assured of eternal life.

111

DAY 33

RELAX Clear the distractions from your head. Close your eyes and take a few deep breaths. Imagine God turning down the volume of these distractions for you, so you can hear what He has to say.

READ

Colossians 3:1–17   Author: Apostle Paul

As you read this passage, underline in your Bible any words or phrases that stand out to you.

REACT

What stands out to you from this passage?

In this passage, Paul used two powerful images: putting things to death and clothing ourselves. According to Paul, what should you put to death (or rid yourself of)? With what should you clothe yourself? Make a list using the spaces below.

Put to Death (or rid myself of) These:	Clothe Myself With These:

Review the two lists. Are any of these commands especially difficult for you to obey?

_____

NOTE: Sometime this week, apply this Bible passage to your life by getting some input from your friends. Choose two or three close friends and ask them in what ways you demonstrate, or don't demonstrate, compassion, humility, patience, kindness, and gentleness. Regardless of what they say, thank them for being honest.

Why do you think Paul said love brings all of these commands together?

_____

RELATE:

Walk through a couple things that you spend your time doing. Write out a way you could "do" each of those things for the glory of God. _For example, when you're at school, don't just do your homework—do it in such a way that your attitude glorifies the God you serve. When you're texting, use it as an opportunity to encourage people so that God is glorified._

RESPOND:

You have the opportunity to worship God through every part of your life (e.g., school, friends, family, sports, etc.) In prayer, think of each part of your life and dedicate it to God. Tell God that you want to glorify Him through every area in your life.

113

DAY 34

RELAX Take a moment to identify the distractions in your head. Take a deep breath. Ask God to help you hear His voice.

READ

Luke 14:25–35   Author: Luke

As you read this passage, underline in your Bible any words or phrases that stand out to you.

REACT

What stands out to you from Jesus' teaching?

What do you think verse 26 means? Does Jesus really mean that we should hate our family?

Why do you think Jesus wants us to count the cost before we follow Him?

NOTE: In ancient times, salt had a variety of different uses, such as flavoring food, preserving meat and dairy products, insuring good health, and creating products like glass and soap. Salt could even be placed on manure to give it nutrients. But if salt lost its saltiness, then it was no longer good for anything; it could actually ruin the manure. Do you understand what Jesus is saying? When Christians stop acting like Christ, they are not even fit for a manure pile.

Why do you think Jesus was so harsh about this?

_____

_____

RELATE:

Many people accept Jesus and then turn away when things get tough. (They never really counted the cost of following Him.) Have you done that in your life?

Are there any ways in which you have compromised when it comes to following Jesus?

RESPOND:

There are two kinds of people: Those who say, "God, I will follow you if...(you keep me healthy, make me rich, etc."), and those who say, "God, I will follow you even if...(I get sick, life falls apart, etc.") Which one are you? Write some "even if" prayers to God.

115

DAY 35

RELAX Clear the distractions from your head. Close your eyes and imagine God waiting to have a conversation with you.

READ

Psalm 103:1–13   Author: David

As you read this passage, underline in your Bible any words or phrases that stand out to you.

Rewrite the psalm in your own words, verse by verse. When you finish, read your prayer out loud to God.

Verse 1

Verse 2

Verse 3

Verse 4

Verse 5

Verse 6 _____

_____

Verse 7 _____

_____

Verse 8 _____

_____

Verse 9 _____

_____

Verse 10 _____

_____

Verse 11 _____

_____

Verse 12 _____

_____

Verse 13 _____

_____

WEEK FIVE

GLOW

How have you lived out what you've learned from God this past week? Where did God show up in your life? Tell at least one story of what God taught you this week through your devotionals, or what happened when you applied what you're learning.

_____

_____

_____

_____

_____

How can you shine with God's light by challenging, encouraging, or inspiring the rest of your group with what God is teaching you? What things are you learning that you hope others in your group are learning, too? What things do you think they most need to know? What could you do together as a group to live out what God is teaching you?

_____

_____

_____

_____

_____

NOTE: This is the last week of the *Life Choices* study; if you are no longer meeting with your group, think of other friends or family members with whom you can share. How can you "glow" and shine God's light on those around you?

SPEAK UP

JOIN THE *TO SAVE A LIFE* COMMUNITY

SPEAK UP
JOIN THE *TO SAVE A LIFE* COMMUNITY

To Save A Life offers you a unique chance to use a movie and a powerful story as a conversation-starter with your friends. It will set you up to talk about things that really matter—like your faith!

Find out how you can get involved and make a difference at ToSaveALifeMovie.com.

Watch the movie with friends and then brainstorm about how you can reach out and help others. Some people are just dying to be heard. If you listen, you might discover a new friend and an opportunity to live an epic life together.

SHARING IS NICE!

- If you liked *To Save A Life* and any of the books or gear, tell your friends about it! They can go to ToSaveALifeMovie.com for updates and links to other cool sites.

- **Artists:** On the movie Web site, we have a place just for you. Share your artwork, and it just might be posted for the world to see!

- **Tell your story**. Post a message on our Facebook page to let us know how the movie impacted you, and how you're making a change on your campus.

TO SAVE A LIFE ONLINE

MOVIE SITE: ToSaveALifeMovie.com

MYSPACE: myspace.com/tosavealifemovie

FACEBOOK: facebook.com/tosavealife

TWITTER: twitter.com/tosavealife

FOR TEEN AND ADULT LEADERS: ToSaveALifeLeaders.com

DEVO2GO: Devo2Go.com

*"Sharing YOUR story
can help others rewrite theirs!"*
—Leeland Mooring (of the band Leeland)

SPREAD THE LOVE!

Life is a journey and it's better to travel with others. Below are a few community activities you can do right where you are:

- Use your Facebook, MySpace, Twitter account, or other social network to do good. Join the *To Save A Life* groups on these sites, follow us, and learn what others are doing to make a difference. You can find the links on the movie Web site.

- Each day, post a note of encouragement, tell someone you care, or leave a friend a message to brighten their day. Invest yourself in others and see how the ripples of your life make an impact on them.

- Start a group on campus or online to bring together people from different backgrounds and communities.

DON'T FORGET!

Go back over your notes in this Student Guide and look for the places where you made comments about things you wanted to do—or do differently. Highlight them. Mark them up so you don't forget your goals, and then begin to live them out!

OTHER TO SAVE A LIFE GEAR

On ToSaveALifeMovie.com, you'll find a link for official gear, like t-shirts, books, jewelry, and more.

See the last few pages in this guide for more information on *To Save A Life* books.

*"When you live out the mission God
created you to do, it's then that
He whispers in response,
'My masterpiece!'"*
—Jim Britts

HANDLING THE
TOUGH STUFF

HANDLING THE TOUGH STUFF

Teens in crisis have trouble functioning in ordinary, day-to-day situations. They have trouble sleeping—or sleep too much. They can't eat—or can't stop eating. They can't feel—or have their emotions stuck wide-open. They can't make decisions—or act impulsively. They hurt themselves—or hurt others.

Help teens resolve crises, and you'll help them avoid the things dealt with in the movie. Below are five steps to help a person in crisis, followed by suggestions about handling four of the crisis situations shown in the movie.

NO MATTER WHAT...

1. Listen carefully until the teen is convinced you understand, care, and want to help.

2. Help the teen involve their parents as soon as possible, even if it will embarrass them. Only when you have reason to believe the parents are a danger should you skip this step.

3. When inviting another person to help, make it clear to everyone that you're *adding* another helper, not *subtracting* yourself. If you don't know how to find more help, call the head counselor or vice principal at their school. Explain who you are and how you know the student. Describe why you think the student is in crisis, particularly if you feel they are a danger to themselves or others.

4. If nothing happens, and you continue to believe the teen is a danger to themselves or others, call local law enforcement or Child Protective Services. Legal jurisdictions can be confusing, so don't give up until you find someone who offers real help. If the process is still taking too long, and you believe the teen is in immediate danger, dial 911 and explain the danger in calm, clear language.

5. Once you know the teen is getting help:
   • Stay close (without hovering).

   • Watch for signs of self-injury. After revealing the root cause of a crisis, some teens feel exposed and go through a heightened risk for behaviors such as cutting, substance abuse, and suicide.

- PRAY.

- Resist the temptation to feed off the emotions associated with the crisis. Don't air dirty laundry under the cover of a "prayer request."

CUTTING + SELF-INJURY

Self-Injurious Behavior (SIB) is repetitive, non-lethal self-injury such as cutting, burning, scratching, hitting, biting, gouging, branding, yanking out hair, and head banging. Eating disorders often accompany SIB. People can do considerable tissue damage and still not be attempting suicide—SIB may be pain management to keep them from killing themselves. But if you believe the damage is a botched suicide, pursue that to its logical conclusion.

If you see physical signs of SIB:

- Ask if the injury is what it looks like. If you don't buy the response, ask if they ever feel like hurting themselves in times of high stress.

- Call in qualified reinforcements quickly. (Refer to #3 in the "No Matter What…" list above.)

- Be aware that people under stress may be tempted to return to self-injury until the underlying causes are resolved.

SUICIDE

Most suicides can be prevented. Most suicidal people hang in the balance between "I really, really want to die" and "I really, really want to live."

Typical risk indicators for suicide:

- A history of developmental problems

- Escalating family problems

- Acute experience of separation and loss

- Feelings of rejection and being unwanted

- Chronic communication problems

- Obvious and abrupt behavioral changes

- Sustained extreme moodiness and withdrawal
- Repeated involvement in high-risk behaviors
- Abuse of alcohol and other drugs
- Medically undiagnosed physical complaints
- Perfectionism
- Despair
- Suicidal notes
- Suicidal language such as, "I'd be better off dead," "You won't have to worry about me much longer," or "No one cares if I'm around, I'll just end it all."
- Giving away treasured objects
- Sudden, unexplained, extravagant emotional elevation in the mood of a chronically depressed person, which may mask a suicidal intention

If you observe some of these behaviors in combination, acknowledge the person's pain and ask if they are frustrated to the point that they have considered hurting themselves. If the answer is "yes," ask if they are actively considering killing themselves.

If you have the slightest reason to believe a person's use of suicidal language may be serious, use this series of questions to explore the level of risk.

S.L.A.P.

S - Specific Details
- Is there a plan? A time? A place? A method?
- On a scale of 1–10 (where 10 = "I'll kill myself as soon as I have an opportunity") where would the teen place themselves? Because they are starting to believe there's nothing to lose, there's a high likelihood they will tell you the truth about their plans.

L - Lethality of Method
- Does the method indicate a clear desire to die (guns, jumping, and hanging are frequently lethal)?

A - Availability of Method

- If the plan includes a method, are those means readily available?

P - Proximity to Helping Resources

- Does the plan involve a location where the teen can't be interrupted?

- Is there anyone they think would want to stop them if they tried? [They may be wrong, but if they can't name anyone who would want to stop their suicide, they are at high risk.]

If you believe the risk is immediate, call for reinforcements immediately. Don't leave the teen alone. Take them to someone who knows what to do. If you don't know such a person, take them to a hospital emergency room. If that's not possible, dial 911 and calmly explain that you are with someone who is a danger to themselves and intends suicide.

Deal with the method. Ask to hold or dispose of the method of choice. Don't use or threaten physical force to take control of a lethal object, but be insistent. Involve the police if necessary.

If you believe the threat is real but not immediate, take the teen to someone who knows how to help people deal with suicidal intentions. If you don't know such a person, take them to the head counselor or vice principal at their school.

Ask them to promise that, from now on, if they feel like harming themselves or ending their life, they will talk to you or someone you agree on who can help get them through the crisis.

HOTLINES:

1-800-Suicide

1-800-273-Talk

1-877-Youthline

SHOOTINGS

Findings by the U. S. Department of Education and the Secret Service offer insights into kids who try to kill fellow students and school personnel:

- School gun violence is rarely sudden. About half of school attackers develop the idea for a month or more; almost all prepare for at least two days.

129

- Most school attackers tell at least one peer they're thinking about an attack. In most cases, at least one adult is concerned by pre-attack behavior.

- More than a third of school attackers have expressed themselves in violent writings prior to their attacks. Artists shouldn't be punished for creativity, but if what a kid says about his writing, drawing, song, or painting doesn't pass the smell test, get help to sort it out.

- More than half of school shootings are motivated by revenge. Most of these attackers feel bullied, threatened, attacked, or injured. Two-thirds tell someone about their grievance, but fewer than one in five threatens his or her target(s) directly.

- Nearly two-thirds of attackers have a documented history of extremely depressed or desperate feelings. More than three-quarters have a history of suicidal expressions. Almost all perceive a major loss prior to the attack.

If you look for an obvious pattern, there is none. School shooters are typically Caucasian males in two-parent homes who do all right in school, don't have histories of violence or cruelty to animals, do have close friends, and associate with social groups, but they struggle to cope with a self-defined loss. Unfortunately, this describes about one in three American high school kids. The Secret Service/Department of Education report concludes, "There is no accurate or useful 'profile' of students who engaged in targeted school violence."

The lesson is both simpler and more complicated than almost anyone anticipated: *Preventing lethal school violence depends on attentive relationships with ordinary schoolboys.* It's simple because potential attackers are in constant contact with people who are capable of spotting signs of potential violence; it's complicated because perceiving it requires focused listening against the backdrop of daily behavior. It's also complicated because it means the unthinkable: Ordinary kids are capable of harming themselves and others.

No one wants to ask a kid if they have thought about suicide or acts of revenge. But if a teen is depressed, bullied, or suffers what they consider a deep loss, we as ministry leaders have to ask the question, and we have to know the kid well enough to know if they are telling the truth.

POST-TRAUMATIC STRESS DISORDER

Post-Traumatic Stress Disorder (PTSD) sometimes develops in the aftermath of witnessing or experiencing bodily injury. PTSD is not universal—most people exposed to traumatic circumstances don't suffer major mental health effects, and those who do tend to recover within a couple of years. But it can be a rough couple of years with flashbacks, vivid memories, intrusive thoughts and nightmares, emotional numbness or hyper-arousal, sleep disturbances, depression, anxiety, headaches, stomach complaints, dizziness, chest pain, irritability, angry outbursts, and feelings of intense guilt. None of this is unusual in the immediate aftermath of trauma. But when symptoms persist beyond a month, mental health professionals may diagnose PTSD. (FYI: About 30 percent of those who spend time in war zones suffer PTSD. Victims of childhood abuse or other prior trauma are somewhat more likely than other people to experience PTSD.)

Full-blown PTSD may be accompanied by addictive or self-destructive behavior, self-doubt, paranoia, psychotic breaks, excessive compliance, fear of intimacy, hopelessness, and despair.

Talking helps, and the sooner the better. Research has proved the effectiveness of talk-based therapy for PTSD. A study of 12,000 schoolchildren following a hurricane found that those who got counseling soon after the storm were doing better after two years than those who didn't. If you suspect PTSD, provide a safe place to talk, and introduce the teen to a mental health professional with experience in PTSD.

FINALLY...

If you are in a position to recognize and identify a crisis, God can use you to get help for a suffering teen. For more information, see:

- Rich Van Pelt and Jim Hancock, *The Youth Worker's Guide to Helping Teenagers in Crisis,* Youth Specialties, 2007

- American Association of Suicidology: www.suicidology.org

- National Institute of Mental Health (http://www.nimh.nih.gov and search under Children and Adolescents)

- Boys and Girls Town 24-hour Hotline: 1-800-448-3000

- National Suicide Prevention Lifeline: www.suicidepreventionlifeline.org